1·2·3 Draw

COOL CARTOON STUFF

A step-by-step guide

by
Steve Barr

Peel Productions, Inc

This book is dedicated to my cousin, Steve Klingler, for all of his help while I was working on this book. We used to draw cartoons together as kids and he has encouraged me to keep going ever since!

-S.B.

Copyright ©2003 Steve Barr.
All rights reserved, including the right of reproduction in whole or in part, in any form.
Published by Peel Productions, Inc.
Manufactured by STONE SAPPHIRE/LF PRODUCTS PTE LTD, China
Printed September 2011 in Shanghai, China

Library of Congress Cataloging-in-Publication Data

Barr, Steve, 1958-
  1-2-3 draw cool cartoon stuff : a step-by-step guide / by Steve Barr.
     v. cm.
  Contents: Before you begin -- Cartooning tips -- Basic shapes and lines -- Sun -- Bone -- Balloon -- Pencils -- Crayon -- Book -- Baseball -- Bat -- Baseball moving -- Beach ball -- Football -- Candle -- Flower -- Trees -- Food.
   ISBN 0-939217-73-2 (pbk. : alk. paper)
  1. Cartooning--Technique--Juvenile literature. [1. Cartooning--Technique. 2. Drawing--Technique.] I. Title: One-two-three draw cool cartoon stuff. II. Title.
   NC1764 .B37 2003
   741.5--dc21   2011-0000125787

This edition produced exclusively for

Books Are Fun
282 Century Place, Suite 2000
Louisville, CO 80027

(888) 293-8114

Table of Contents

Before you begin

You will need the following supplies:

- Pencil (or pencils!)
- Eraser
- Pencil sharpener
- Ruler
- LOTS of paper
- Colored pencils, markers or crayons
- Good light
- Comfortable place to draw
- Your imagination!

Now, let's begin!

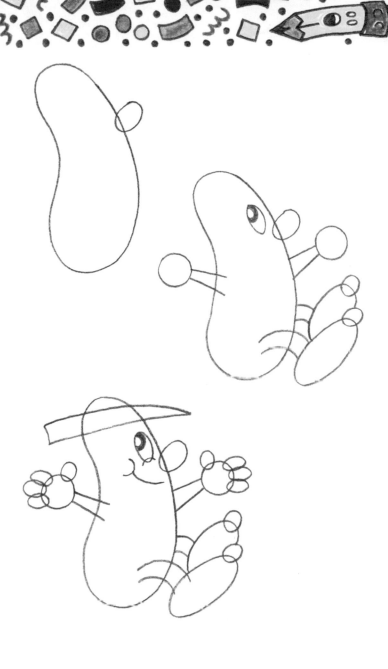

NO rules!

The coolest part of drawing cartoons is there are NO rules! Cartoons are simple drawings using basic shapes and lines to create a funny picture.

Use this book as a basic guide to show you how to make inanimate objects come to life. Look at the example on this page. It's just a rounded blob at first. But by adding a few lines and shapes, it turns into a fun cartoon guy wearing a hat.

Sketch, doodle, play!

Sketch lightly at first, in case you want to make changes later. Experiment. It's your creation. It the instructions tell you to draw a round oval nose and you feel like drawing a triangular nose, draw it. Try different shapes and lines. Color your cartoons any color you wish. Develop a style of your own. If your drawings make you laugh or giggle, congratulations! You are becoming a cartoonist!

Doodle! Play! If you end up creating a cartoon character that makes you rich and famous, please remember to invite me to your amusement park when you build it. I love riding on roller coasters almost as much as I love drawing cartoons!

Cartooning tips:

1 Draw lightly at first-SKETCH, so you can erase extra lines.
2 Practice, practice, practice! You will get better and your cartoons will get funnier.
3 Have FUN cartooning!

Basic Shapes and Lines

Here are the basic shapes and lines
you will use to draw cool cartoons.

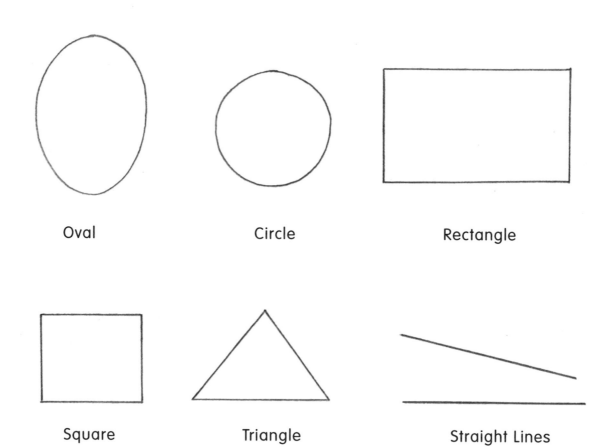

Oval   Circle   Rectangle

Square   Triangle   Straight Lines

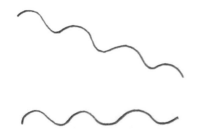      

Squiggly Lines   Curved Lines   Wave

Sun

Let's start with something easy! Let's draw a cartoon sun.

1 Lightly sketch an oval for the face. Draw a slightly curved line to begin the top of the sunglasses. Draw two curved lines for the smiling mouth.

2 Add two curved lines to complete the sunglasses.

3 Draw jagged lines connecting around the outside of the oval.

4 LOOK carefully at the final drawing. Go over and darken the lines. Add color. Leave little circles of white in his glasses to look like light is reflecting off the lenses.

Congratulations!
You just drew a cartoon sun!

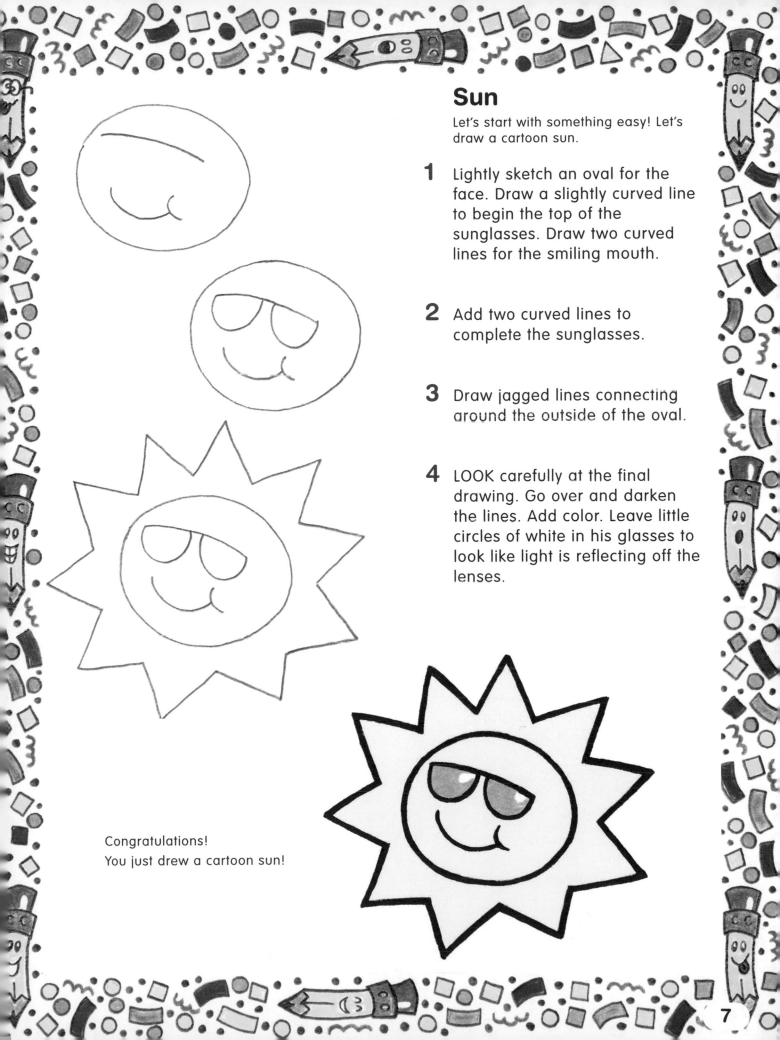

Bone

You can turn almost anything into a cartoon character. Let's make a bone come to life!

1 Lightly sketch two circles touching each other. Add a long curved line at the bottom of each circle.

2 Sketch two more circles touching the bottom of each line.

3 Draw two ovals for eyes. Darken the bottom part of each eye. Draw four curved lines for a smiling mouth.

4 LOOK at the final drawing! Darken the final lines. Add a little color.

What a friendly looking bone! Good job!

Balloon

Let's try a little more complicated drawing. Let's draw a cartoon balloon!

1 Sketch a large circle and a small overlapping circle at the bottom of it.

2 Sketch two ovals for eyes. Draw two curved lines for a mouth.

3 Draw a curved line at the bottom of each eye. Add another curved line under the mouth. Draw a curved line over the small bottom circle.

9

4 Starting at the top, draw two curved lines inside each eye oval for eyeballs. Add two curved lines to complete the neck.

5 Darken part of the eyeballs. Add another curved line inside the mouth. Add a long curving line for a string.

6 LOOK at the final drawing! Erase extra sketch lines that you don't need. Darken the final lines. Add color.

Nice balloon, although he seems a little flighty!

Pencil talking

Here's a fun one. Let's make a pencil come to life! Use your ruler to make really straight lines.

1 Sketch a small rectangle on top of a long triangle.

2 Draw three straight lines on top to make an eraser. Draw two straight lines to make a triangle shape on the bottom.

3 Starting at the top, draw two ovals inside the upper rectangle. Add straight lines to make triangle shapes at the bottom and tip of the pencil.

4 Draw two ovals with a small circle inside each for eyes. Add a curved line for a smile.

5 Starting at the top, draw a straight line in the center of the pencil. Darken part of each eye. Add another curved line to the mouth. Draw another straight line below the mouth.

6 LOOK at the final drawing! Erase any extra lines. Darken the final lines and add color.

Cool cartoon pencil.
He looks sharp!

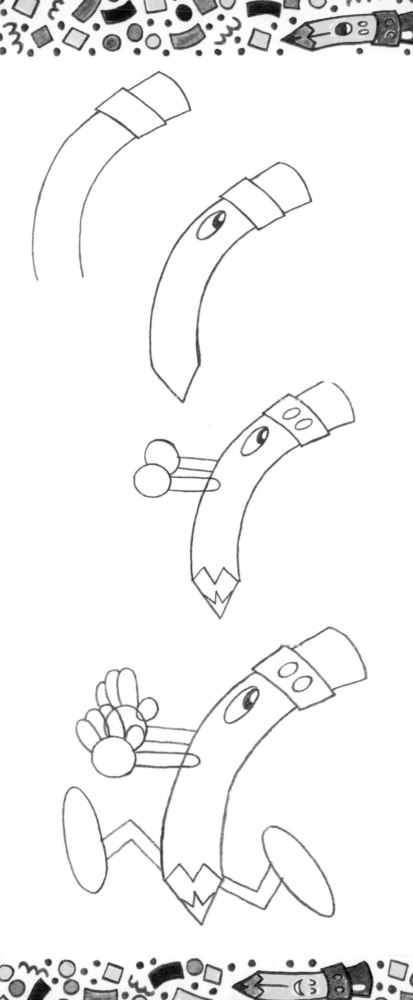

Pencil running

Remember how we said there are no rules in cartooning? Even though a pencil is straight, you can bend it in a cartoon to show motion.

1 Draw two long curved lines. Add a curved line on top. Draw a bent rectangle near the top.

2 Draw an oval for the eye. Draw the eyeball, darken part of it.

3 Draw two small ovals inside the bent rectangle. Draw straight and curved lines for the arms. Sketch ovals for hands. Draw jagged lines to add triangle shapes to the bottom.

4 Sketch long curved lines for fingers on each hand. Draw straight lines for legs. Sketch ovals for feet.

5 Starting at the top, draw two squiggly lines and a tear drop behind the pencil. Draw a long curved line down the side of the pencil. Draw a curved mouth and darken it. Put two curved lines under her front foot.

6 LOOK at the final drawing! Erase extra sketch lines. Darken the final lines. Add color.

Look at your pencil run! I don't think she wants to go to school today.

Crayon

Let's make a friend for your pencil character. Pencils and crayons go together pretty well, so let's bring a crayon to life! Use your ruler to make the rectangle really straight.

1 Draw a long rectangle. Add two curved lines to each side on the bottom. Connect the curved lines with a straight line.

2 Add two straight lines to the top and bottom of the rectangle. Sketch an oval for an eye.

3 Draw an oval for an eyeball. Darken part of it. Add a curved line, to the left side of the rectangle, for the nose.

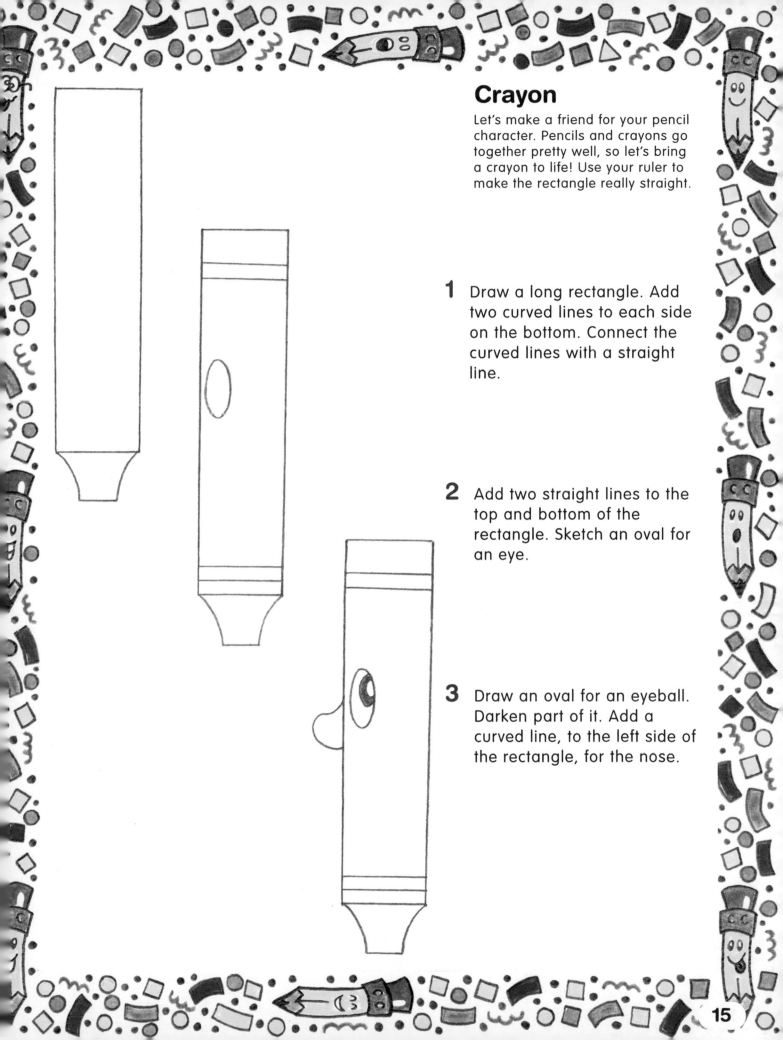

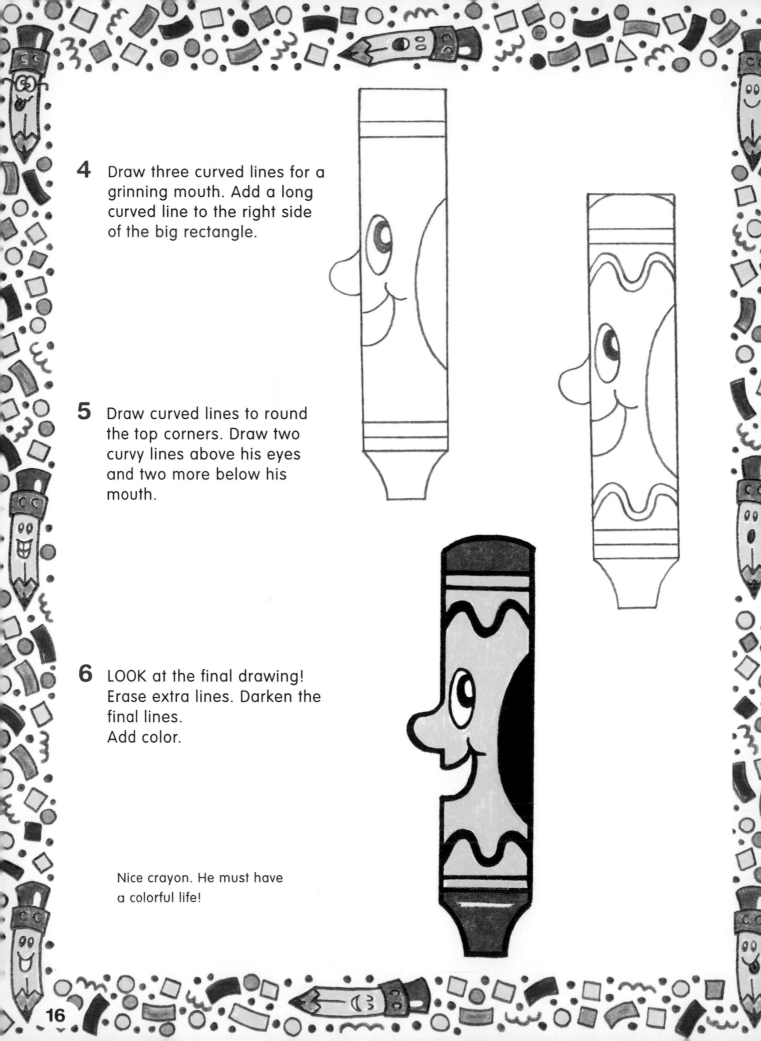

4 Draw three curved lines for a grinning mouth. Add a long curved line to the right side of the big rectangle.

5 Draw curved lines to round the top corners. Draw two curvy lines above his eyes and two more below his mouth.

6 LOOK at the final drawing! Erase extra lines. Darken the final lines. Add color.

Nice crayon. He must have a colorful life!

Book

Since we are drawing school supplies, let's draw a cartoon book. Use your ruler to make the lines really straight.

1 Draw a large rectangle. Draw two ovals for eyes. Darken part of each eye. Draw three curved lines for a smiling mouth.

2 Add six straight lines behind the rectangle to make the book look three-dimensional. Add two more curved mouth lines.

3 Draw three short, curved lines above the rectangle. Add another short curved line to the right of the bottom of the rectangle. Add two curved lines inside the bottom of the mouth and darken the inside of the mouth.

4 Draw three straight lines, touching the inside curved lines, to make pages in the book. Draw two straight lines for arms, on each side of the book.

5 Sketch ovals and curved lines for hands and fingers.

6 LOOK at the final drawing! Erase extra sketch lines. Darken the final lines. Add color.

Wow! He looks like a fun book!

Baseball

During recess your cartoon friends will probably want to play ball. Let's draw a cartoon baseball for them.

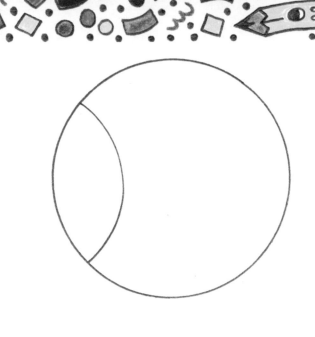

1 Draw a circle. (It's okay to trace a round object. But remember no rules! It's also okay if your circle turns out a little wobbly!) Add a curved line inside the circle.

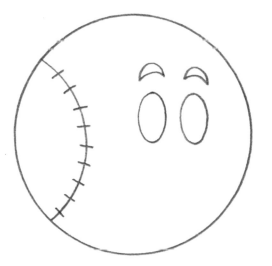

2 Add short straight lines to the curved line for stitches. Draw two ovals for eyes. Draw two curved lines above each eye for eyebrows.

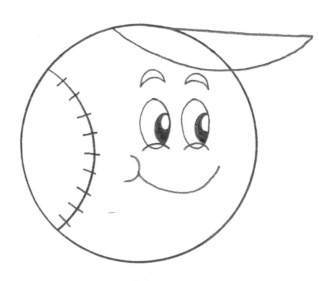

3 Draw a straight line and a curved line to begin the hat. Add an oval inside each eye, for the eyeball. Darken part of it. Draw a short curved line below each eye. Draw two curved lines to begin the mouth.

4 Draw a curved line above the ball for the top of the hat. Draw a curved line to make the bottom of the mouth.

5 Draw a small circle on the top of the hat. Draw a curved line inside the hat. Add a curved line inside the mouth for teeth.

6 LOOK at the final drawing! Erase extra sketch lines. Darken the final lines. Add color.

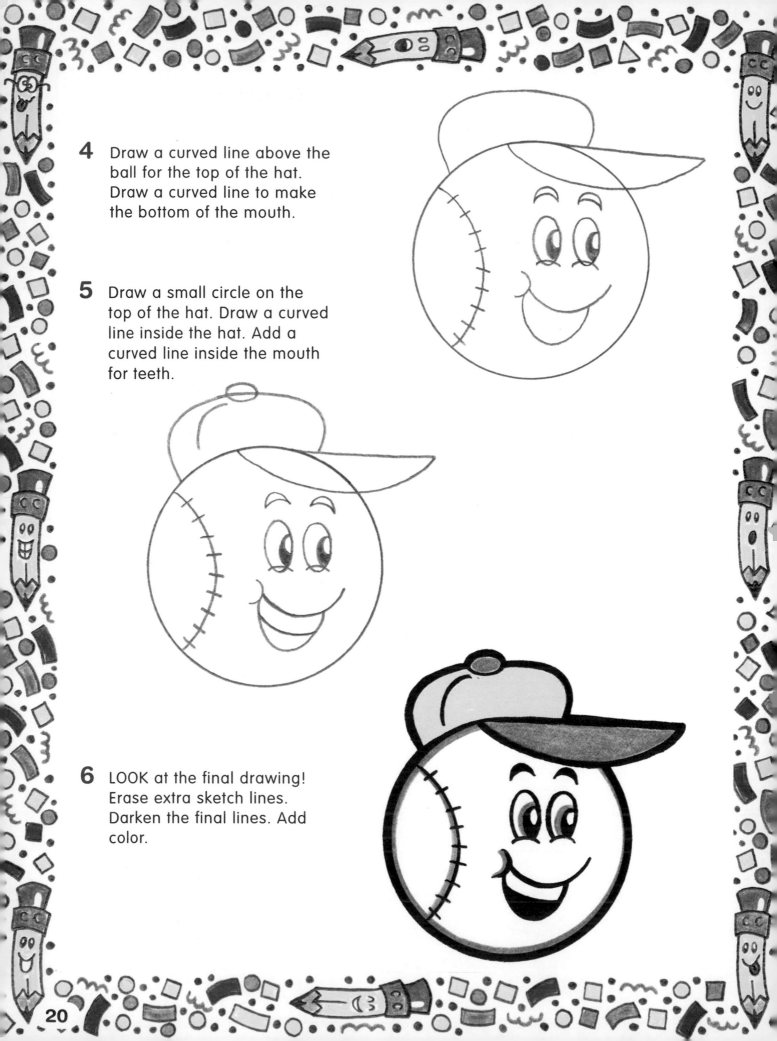

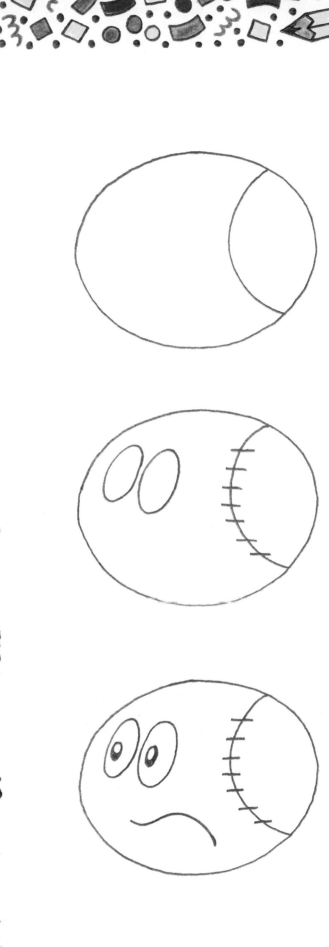

Baseball moving

Remember the bent pencil running on page 13? You can bend an object to make it look like it's moving or you can stretch a cartoon character to show movement. Let's draw a moving baseball.

1 Sketch an oval. Draw a curved line inside the oval.

2 Sketch two ovals for eyes. Add straight lines to the curved line for stitching.

3 Draw an oval inside each eye. Darken part of it. Look at the mouth. Draw a curved line for the mouth.

4 Add two more curved lines to the bottom of his mouth.

5 Darken the center of the mouth. Add five straight lines coming off the back of the ball to show movement.

6 LOOK at the final drawing! Darken the final lines. Add color.

Great baseball! It looks like it is screaming out of the ballpark!

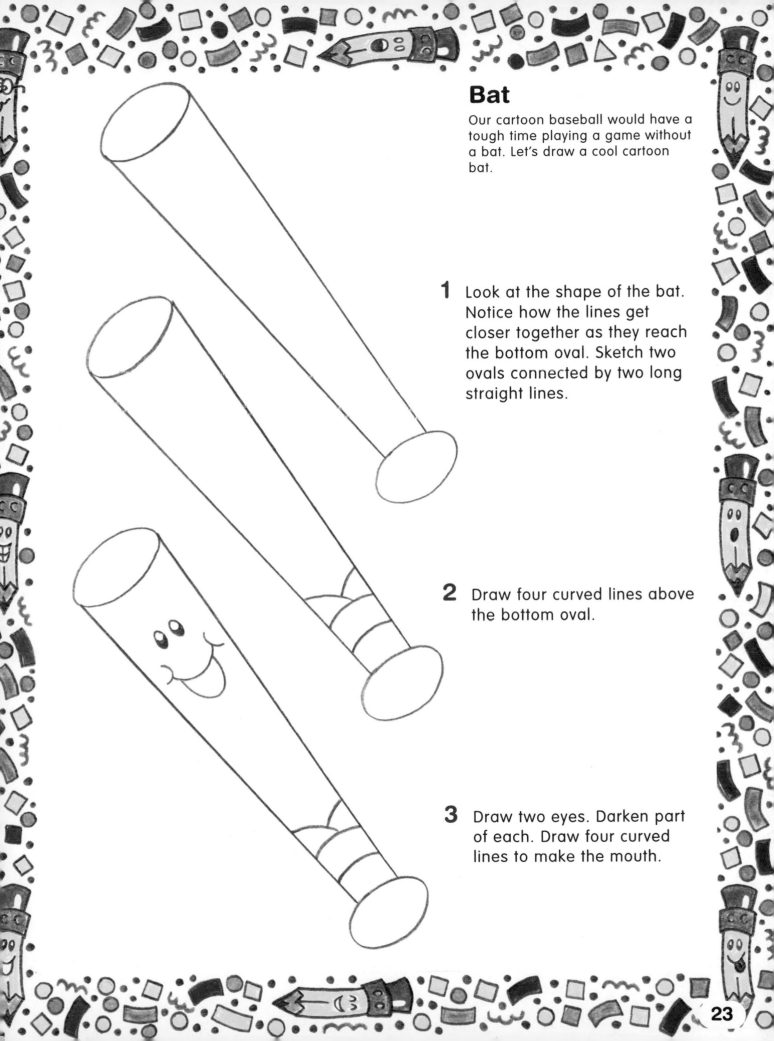

Bat

Our cartoon baseball would have a tough time playing a game without a bat. Let's draw a cool cartoon bat.

1 Look at the shape of the bat. Notice how the lines get closer together as they reach the bottom oval. Sketch two ovals connected by two long straight lines.

2 Draw four curved lines above the bottom oval.

3 Draw two eyes. Darken part of each. Draw four curved lines to make the mouth.

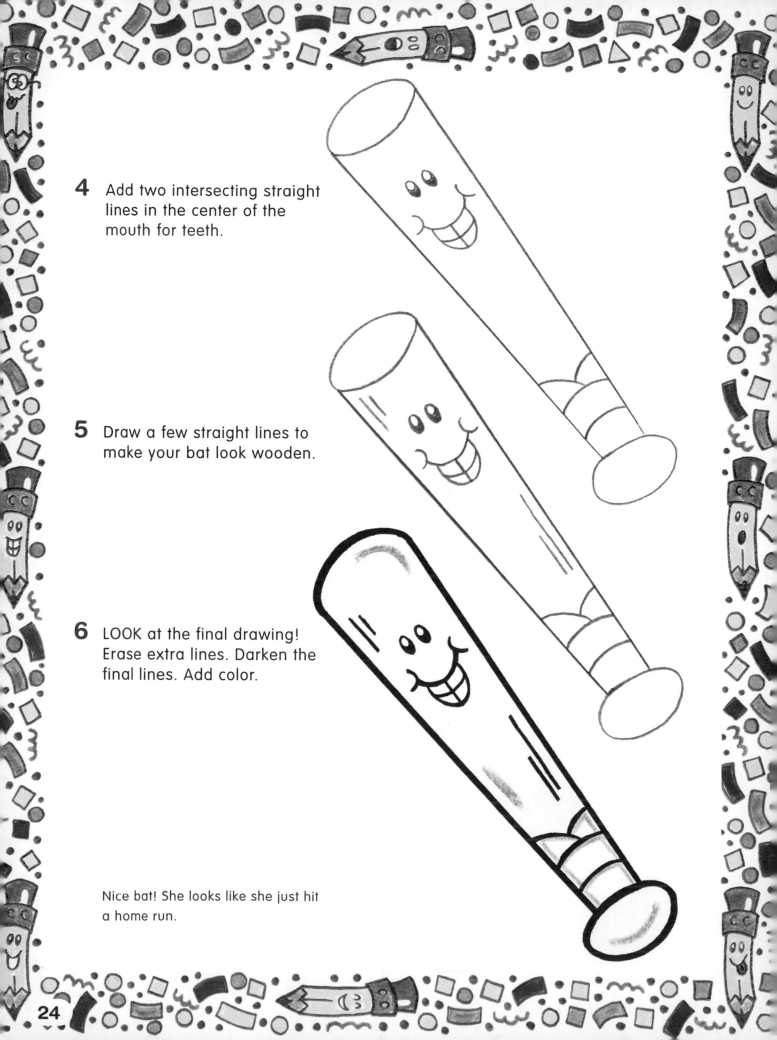

4 Add two intersecting straight lines in the center of the mouth for teeth.

5 Draw a few straight lines to make your bat look wooden.

6 LOOK at the final drawing! Erase extra lines. Darken the final lines. Add color.

Nice bat! She looks like she just hit a home run.

Bowling ball

Let's draw a bowling ball with bowling shoes.

1 Draw a circle. Sketch three small ovals at the top of the circle. Draw two eyeballs. Darken part of each.

2 Draw a curved line inside each oval. Draw two curved lines under the eyeballs. Draw two curved lines for a mouth.

3 Draw an oval around each eyeball for eyes. Draw two straight lines on the outside of the eyes for eyelashes. Draw two connecting curved lines on each side of the bottom, to begin the two shoes.

4 Add curved lines on each foot to turn them into bowling shoes.

5 Draw two curved lines across the toe of each shoe for laces.

6 LOOK at the final drawing! Erase extra lines. Darken the final lines. Add color.

She's a winner! Bet she rolls right over her competition.

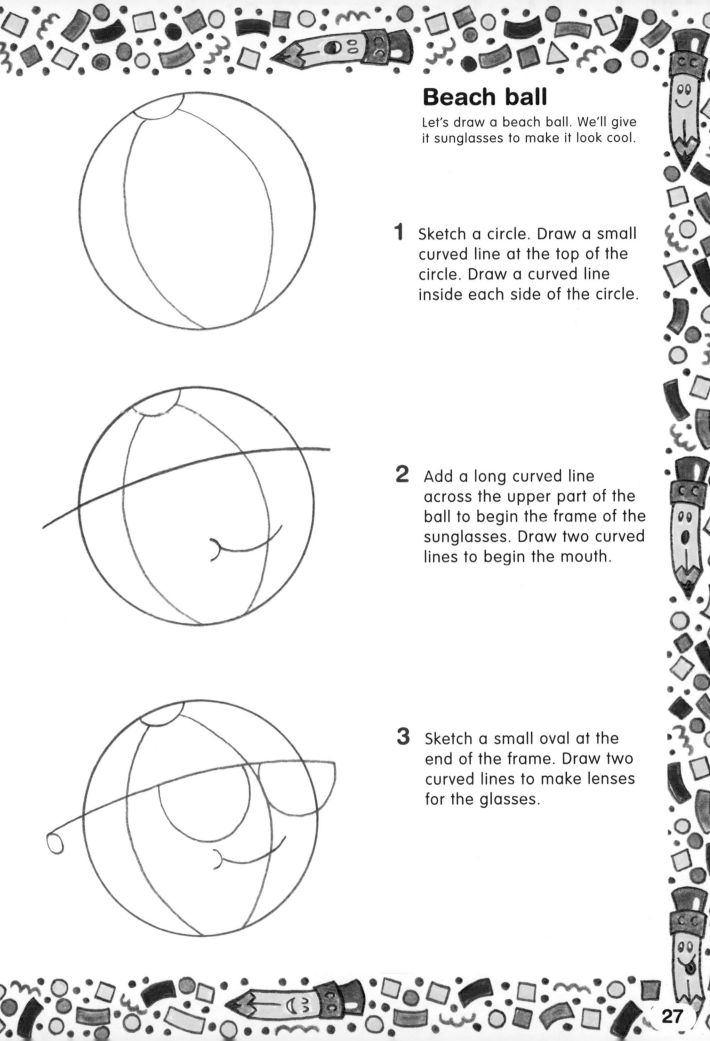

Beach ball

Let's draw a beach ball. We'll give it sunglasses to make it look cool.

1 Sketch a circle. Draw a small curved line at the top of the circle. Draw a curved line inside each side of the circle.

2 Add a long curved line across the upper part of the ball to begin the frame of the sunglasses. Draw two curved lines to begin the mouth.

3 Sketch a small oval at the end of the frame. Draw two curved lines to make lenses for the glasses.

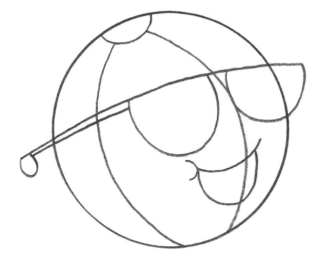

4 Add a curved line to finish the frames of the glasses. Draw another curved line for the mouth.

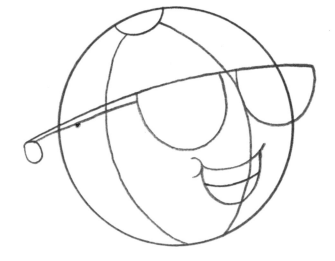

5 Put a curved line inside the center of the mouth for teeth.

6 LOOK at the final drawing! Erase extra sketch lines. Darken the final lines. Add color.

Cool beach ball! Good job!

American football

Let's draw a tough-guy football this time.

1 Sketch a football shaped oval. Draw two eyeballs. Darken part of each. Draw a long curved line for the mouth.

2 Add two curved lines to the top of the football and two to the bottom. Draw two squiggly lines above the eyes for eyebrows. Add two straight lines to the mouth.

3 Draw a long curved line from the top to the bottom, going between the eyes. Add two straight lines in the center of the mouth, for teeth.

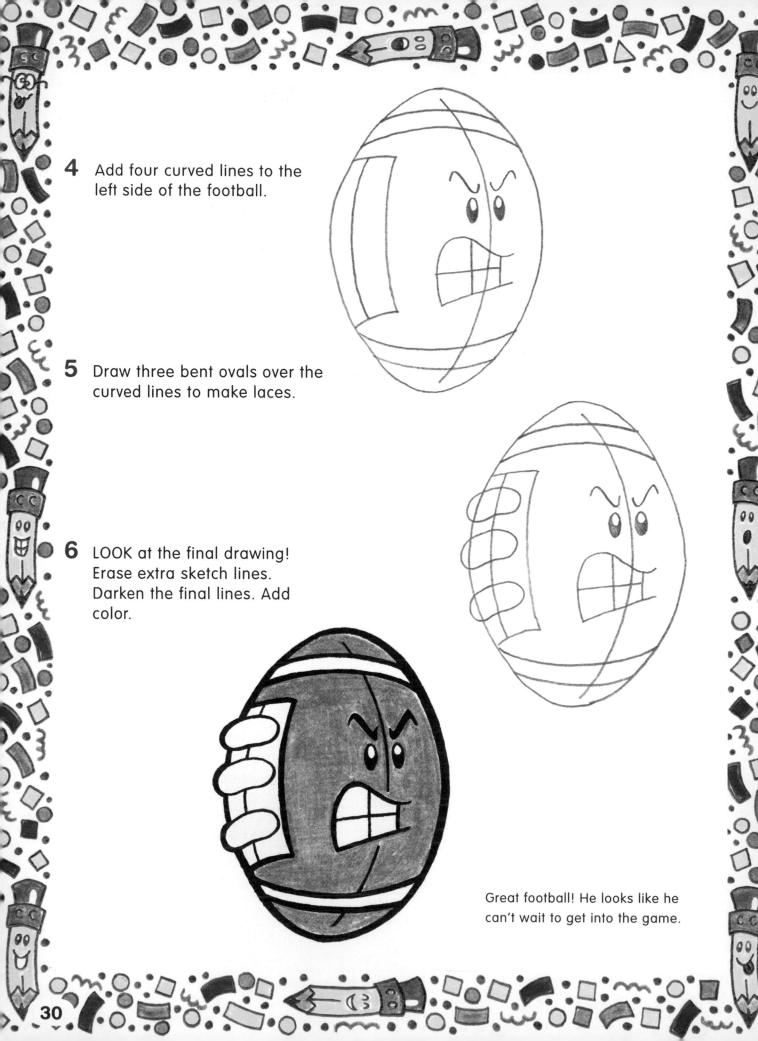

4 Add four curved lines to the left side of the football.

5 Draw three bent ovals over the curved lines to make laces.

6 LOOK at the final drawing! Erase extra sketch lines. Darken the final lines. Add color.

Great football! He looks like he can't wait to get into the game.

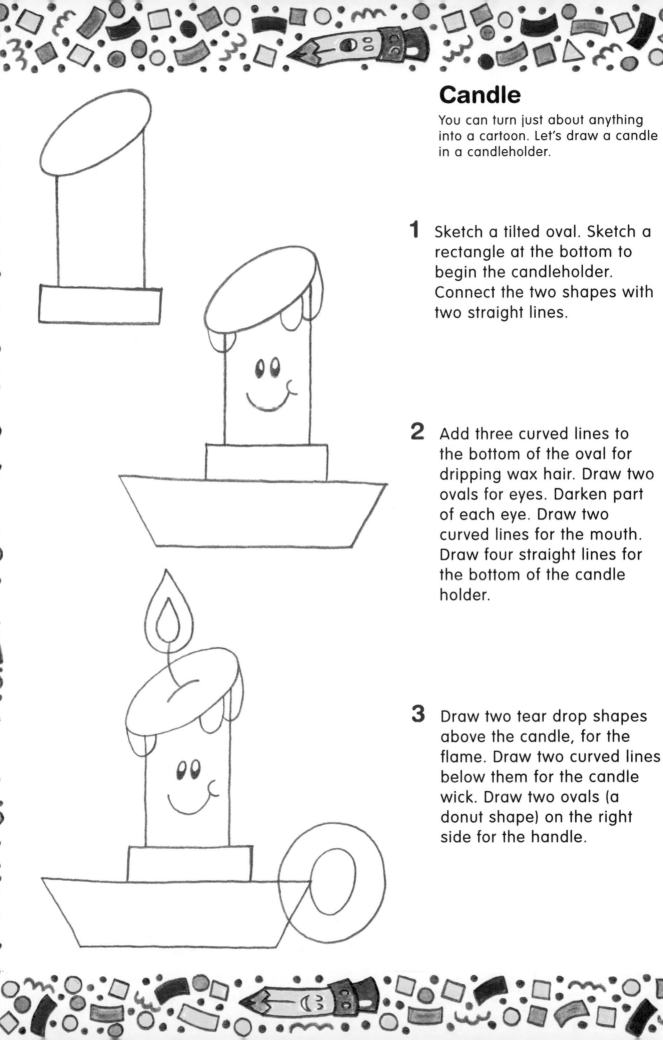

Candle

You can turn just about anything into a cartoon. Let's draw a candle in a candleholder.

1 Sketch a tilted oval. Sketch a rectangle at the bottom to begin the candleholder. Connect the two shapes with two straight lines.

2 Add three curved lines to the bottom of the oval for dripping wax hair. Draw two ovals for eyes. Darken part of each eye. Draw two curved lines for the mouth. Draw four straight lines for the bottom of the candle holder.

3 Draw two tear drop shapes above the candle, for the flame. Draw two curved lines below them for the candle wick. Draw two ovals (a donut shape) on the right side for the handle.

31

4 Sketch two straight lines and a circle, on each side of the candle, for arms and hands.

5 Add curved lines to each hand for fingers.

6 LOOK at the final drawing! Erase extra sketch lines. Darken the final lines. Add color.

Cool candle! She looks bright!

Flower

You can even make plants into cartoon characters. Let's draw a cute cartoon flower in a pot.

1 Sketch a circle. Draw two ovals for eyes. Darken part of each eye. Draw six straight lines coming out of the sides of the circle.

2 Draw curved lines connecting the ends of each of the straight lines. Add two small curved lines for a mouth.

3 Draw two curved lines at the bottom for the stem. Sketch an oval on each side of the curved lines for two leaves.

4 Look at the shape of the flower pot. Draw the straight and curved lines you see to shape the pot.

5 Draw squiggly lines inside each of the petals. Draw a curved line inside each leaf.

6 LOOK closely at the final drawing! Erase extra sketch lines. Darken the final lines. Add color.

Fun flower! Great job!

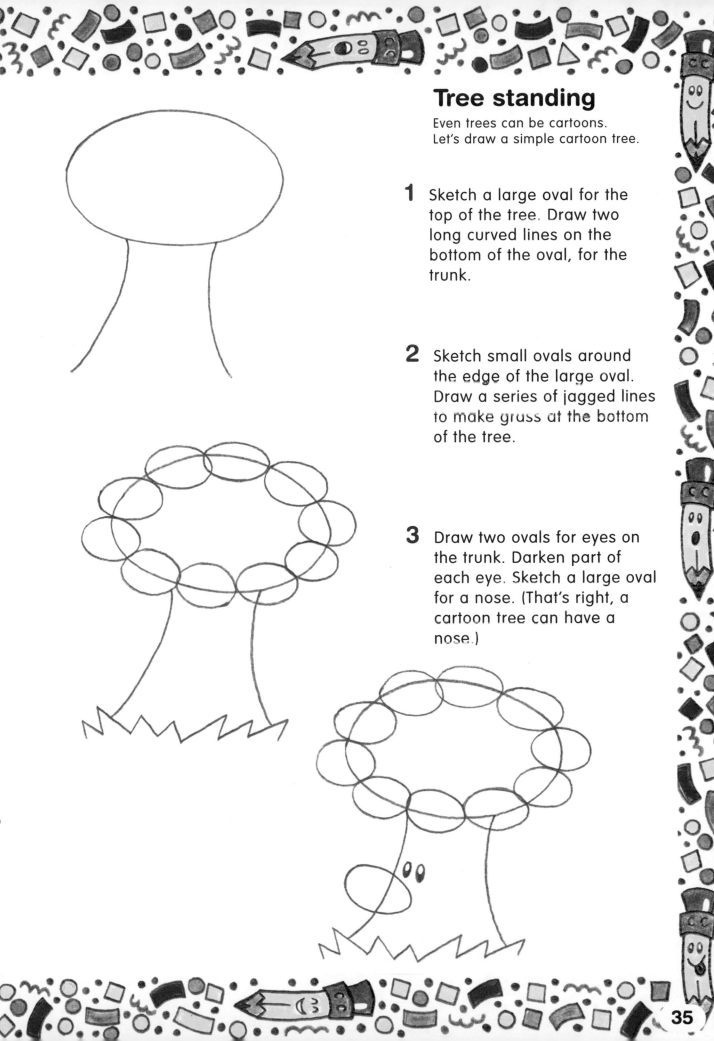

Tree standing

Even trees can be cartoons.
Let's draw a simple cartoon tree.

1 Sketch a large oval for the top of the tree. Draw two long curved lines on the bottom of the oval, for the trunk.

2 Sketch small ovals around the edge of the large oval. Draw a series of jagged lines to make grass at the bottom of the tree.

3 Draw two ovals for eyes on the trunk. Darken part of each eye. Sketch a large oval for a nose. (That's right, a cartoon tree can have a nose.)

4 Draw two curved lines for a mouth.

5 Draw short curved lines on the nose and side of the trunk, to make the tree look like wood.

6 LOOK at the final drawing! Erase extra sketch lines. Darken the final lines. Add color.

Great job!
What a fine looking tree!

Tree in action

Let's draw another tree. This time we will turn some of his branches into arms and hands.

1 Draw a puffy cloud shape. Draw two long curved lines for the trunk.

2 Sketch a long, thin rectangle to each side of the trunk for arms. Draw straight lines to shape the fingers. Add two small curved lines on the bottom of your tree.

3 Add a few small curved lines inside the cloud shape for leaves. Draw two ovals for eyes. Darken part of each oval. Add jagged curved lines at the bottom for grass.

4 Draw two curved lines for a mouth. Add a few short, curved lines to the trunk to make it look like wood.

5 Add two curved lines to the bottom of the mouth.

6 LOOK at the final drawing! Erase extra sketch lines. Darken the final lines. Add color.

Terrific tree! Try drawing a bunch of cartoon trees to make a cartoon forest!

Apple

Food is always fun to draw. Let's draw a simple cartoon apple.

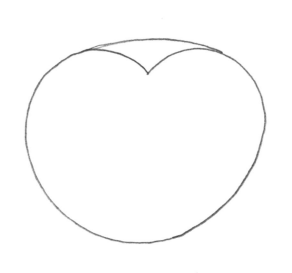

1 Sketch an oval. Draw two curved lines at the top.

2 Draw two curved lines coming out of the top for a stem. Draw two connecting ovals for eyes.

3 Sketch a small circle at the top of the stem. Draw two small ovals inside each eye for the eyeballs.

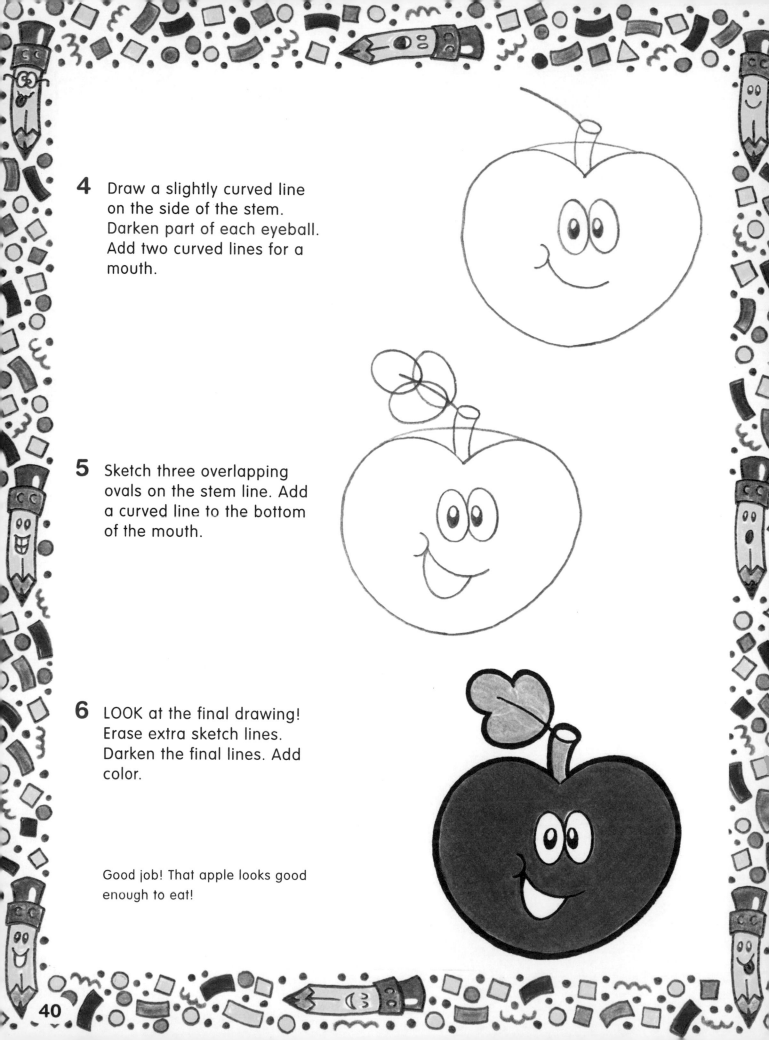

4   Draw a slightly curved line on the side of the stem. Darken part of each eyeball. Add two curved lines for a mouth.

5   Sketch three overlapping ovals on the stem line. Add a curved line to the bottom of the mouth.

6   LOOK at the final drawing! Erase extra sketch lines. Darken the final lines. Add color.

Good job! That apple looks good enough to eat!

Ice cream cone

One of my favorite foods is ice cream! Let's draw a cartoon ice cream cone.

1 Sketch a circle. Draw two curved lines connecting at the bottom for the cone.

2 Draw four connecting curved lines below the circle.

3 Draw two short curved lines for happy eyes. Draw two curved lines for a mouth.

4 Add a curved line to the mouth. Draw a straight line in the center of it to make a tongue.

5 Draw short crossed lines inside the cone to give it texture.

6 LOOK at the final drawing! Erase extra sketch lines. Darken the final lines. Add color. Put a few brightly colored rectangles on your ice cream cone to make jimmies!

Yummy looking ice cream cone! He looks like a party just waiting to happen!

Cake

You can't have a party without a cake. Let's draw a slice of cake to go with our ice cream.

1 Sketch a triangle for the top of the cake. Draw two curved lines below the bottom corners of the triangle.

2 Draw connecting curved lines for icing. Add a curved line to the bottom of the cake slice. Draw lines for the candlestick.

3 Draw two teardrop shapes (one inside the other) for a flame. Draw two ovals for eyes. Darken part of each eye. Draw two curved lines for the mouth.

4 Draw a "S" shaped line, above the flame for smoke. Draw two large curved lines below the slice of cake, to make a plate.

5 LOOK at the final drawing! Erase extra sketch lines. Darken the final lines. Add color.

Cool drawing! That really takes the cake! You are talented!

Hot chocolate

After cake and ice cream I love to pamper myself with a cup of hot chocolate. Let's draw one.

1 Look carefully at this drawing. Sketch two ovals connected by two straight lines.

2 Draw a small oval inside a larger oval for the cup's handle.

3 Draw two small ovals for eyes. Darken part of each eye. Draw three curved lines for a mouth.

4 Add two more lines to the smiling mouth. Draw a curved line inside the top oval. Add a squiggly line for steam.

5 LOOK at the final drawing! Erase extra sketch lines. Darken the final lines. Add color.

Great cup of hot chocolate.
He sure has a friendly-looking mug!

Cool beverage

Let's draw a cool beverage now. Milk shake or a soda? Your choice.

1 Sketch a large oval on top. Sketch a smaller oval below. Draw two straight lines to connect the two ovals.

2 Add a curved line around the top of the large oval for a lid. Draw a curved line inside the lower oval.

3 Draw two curved lines coming out of the top for a straw. Draw two ovals for eyes. Darken part of each eye. Draw a curved line for a mouth.

4 Add a small circle to connect the ends of the straw. Draw two curved lines on each side for arms. Sketch small ovals for wrists, hands, and fingers. Add three curved lines to the bottom of the mouth.

5 LOOK at the final drawing! Erase extra sketch lines. Darken the final lines. Add color.

Cool drink!

Banana

Let's draw something healthy for a change. How about a banana?

1 Sketch a hot dog shape.

2 Draw two eyes. Darken part of each. Draw two curved lines for a mouth.

3 Add another curved line to the bottom of the mouth. Draw two curved lines coming out each side of the banana, to begin the peel. Make the top two lines connect to each other.

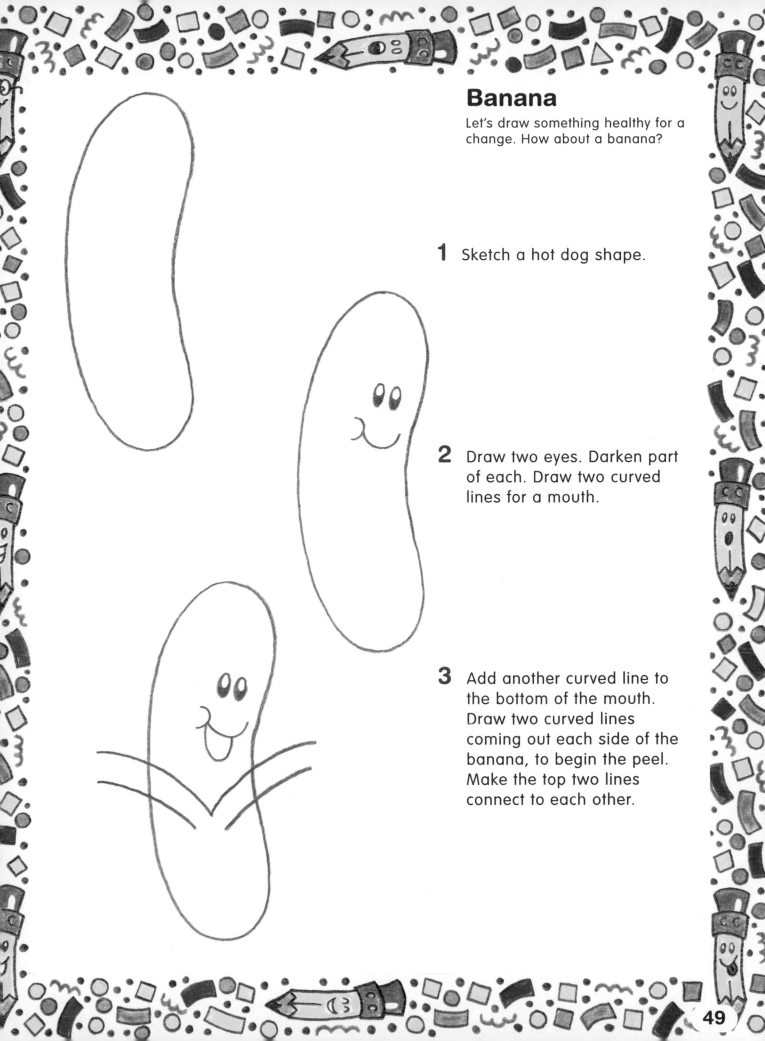

4 Add a curved line inside the mouth, for teeth. Add curved lines on each side to finish the peel.

5 Draw a curved line along the top side of the banana. Draw another one along the bottom side of the peel.

6 LOOK at the final drawing! Erase extra sketch lines. Darken the final lines. Add color.

Wow! That banana has real a-peel!

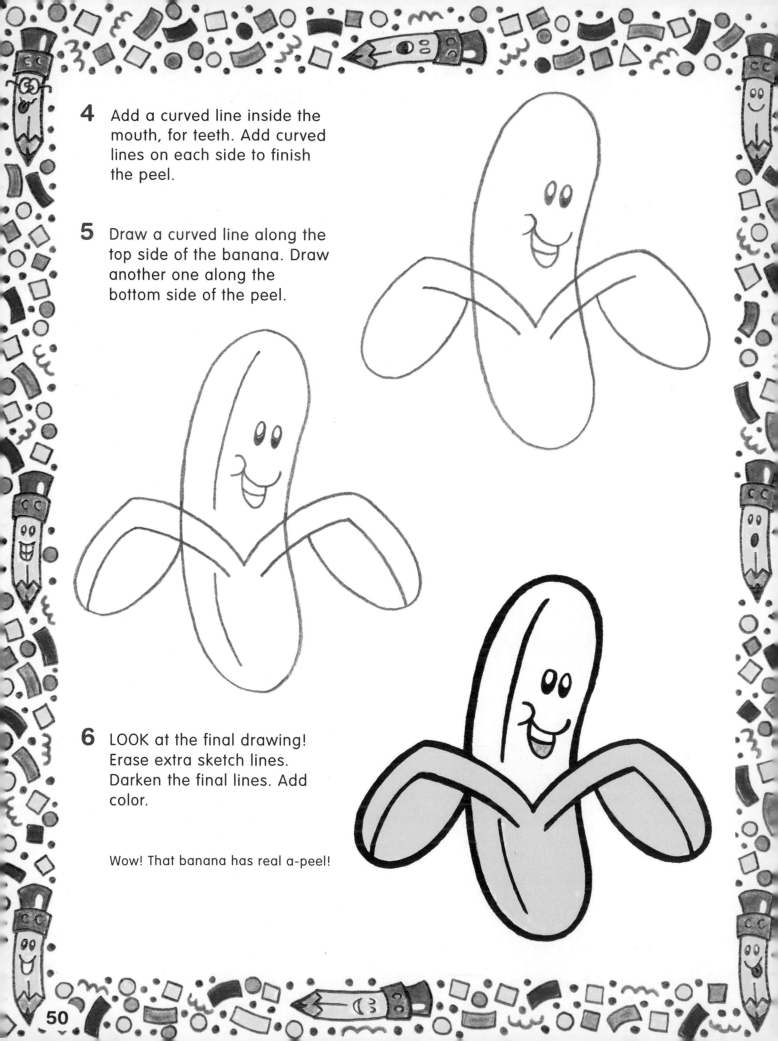

Hamburger

Let's draw a cartoon hamburger on a sesame bun.

1 Sketch an oval. Draw two curved lines in the center for happy eyes.

2 Draw three curved lines to make a smiling mouth.

3 Add a series of curved lines below each side of the oval for lettuce.

4 Draw two long curved lines for the bottom of the hamburger bun.

5 Add small ovals above the eyes for sesame seeds.

6 LOOK at the final drawing! Darken the final lines. Add color.

Nice hamburger!
He has cute buns!

Hot dog

Hamburgers and hot dogs go together. Let's draw a cartoon hot dog.

1 Draw a hot dog shape. Sketch another hot dog shape to the left side for part of a bun. Draw a curved line on the right side for the other part of the bun.

2 Draw a small curved line on top to connect the two bun parts. Draw two small ovals for eyes. Darken part of each eye. Draw three curved lines for a mouth.

3 Draw two straight lines for arms, on each side. Sketch an oval and a circle at the end of the lines for hands.

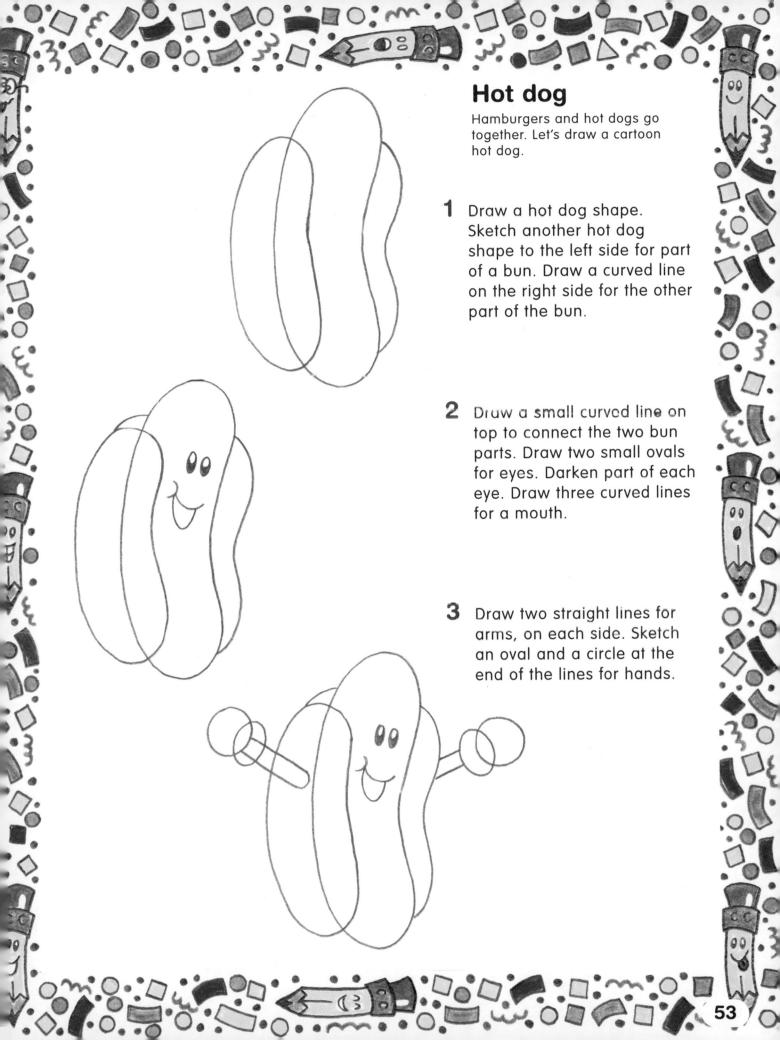

4 Sketch small ovals at the end of each hand for fingers. Draw curved lines for legs. Add an oval and a curved line for two shoes.

5 Draw curved lines inside the shoes to make shoe laces. Add a curved line to the bottom of each shoe.

6 LOOK at the final drawing! Erase extra sketch lines. Darken the final lines. Add color.

What a hot dog! Great job!

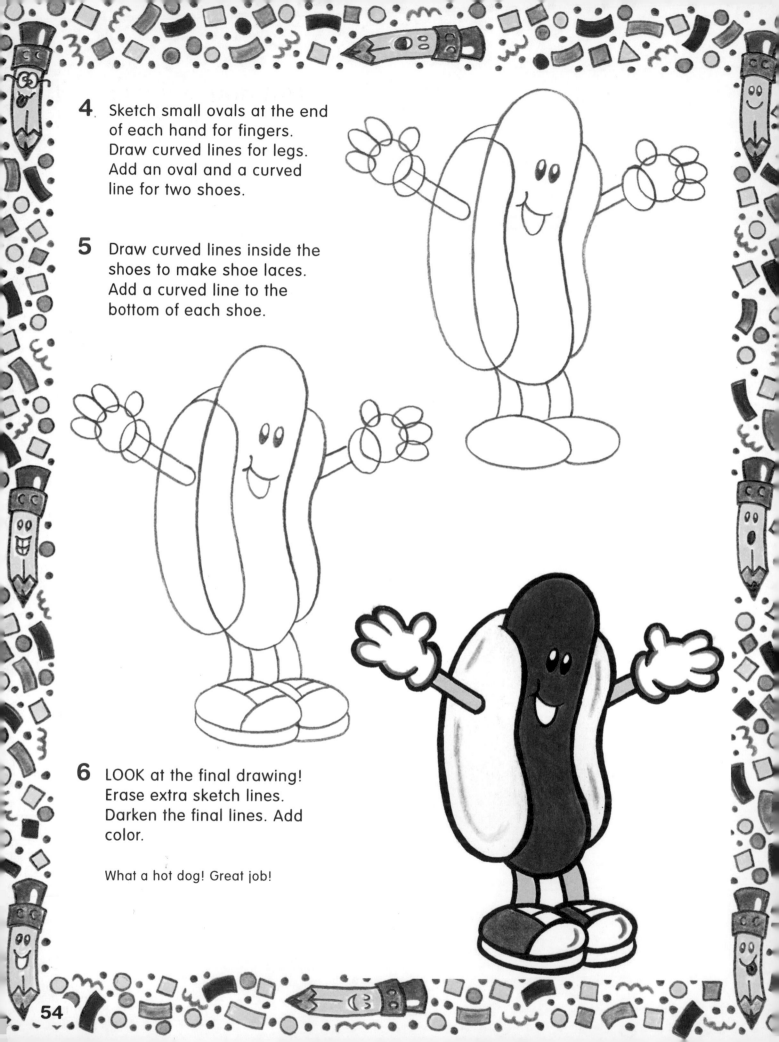

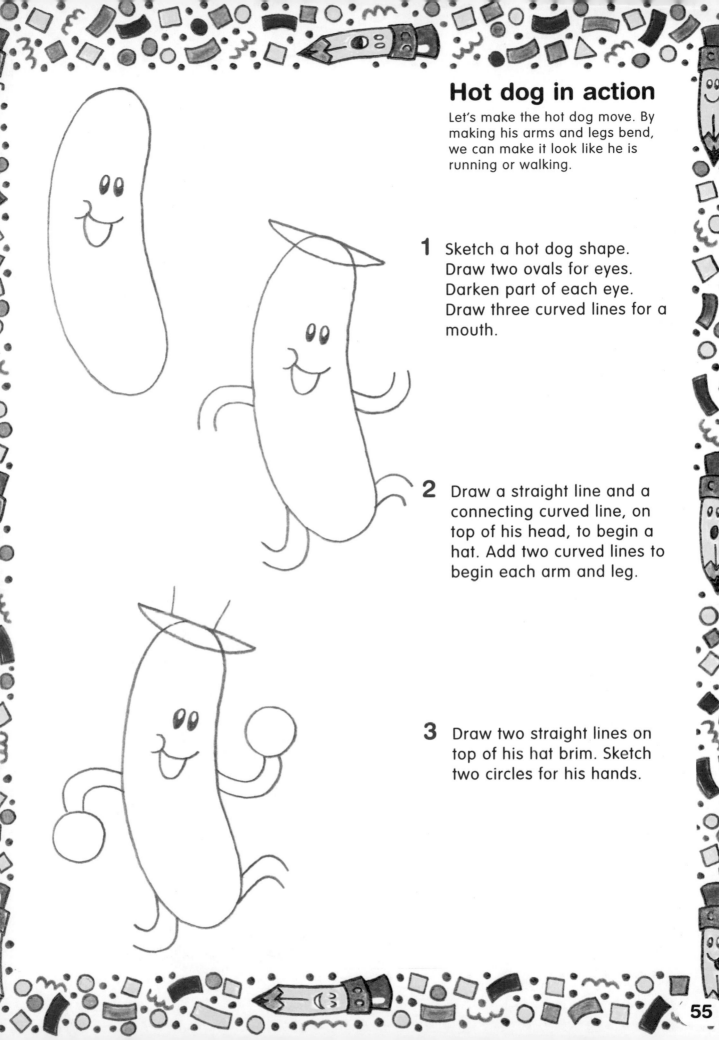

Hot dog in action

Let's make the hot dog move. By making his arms and legs bend, we can make it look like he is running or walking.

1 Sketch a hot dog shape. Draw two ovals for eyes. Darken part of each eye. Draw three curved lines for a mouth.

2 Draw a straight line and a connecting curved line, on top of his head, to begin a hat. Add two curved lines to begin each arm and leg.

3 Draw two straight lines on top of his hat brim. Sketch two circles for his hands.

4 Draw two curved lines, connecting to the straight lines, to finish the hat. Sketch two ovals for feet.

5 Sketch small ovals for fingers and a thumb on each hand.

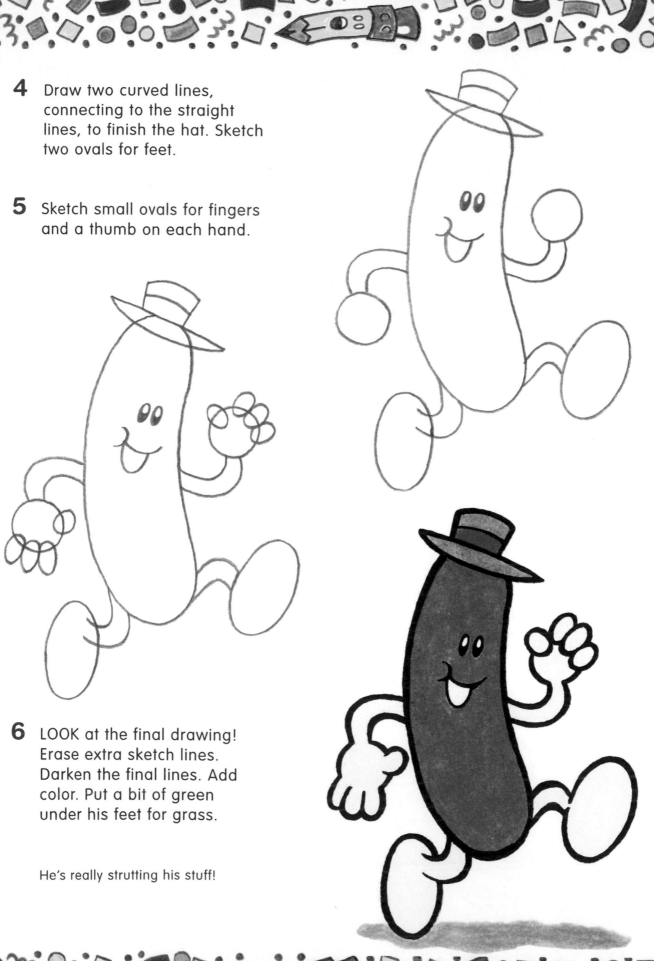

6 LOOK at the final drawing! Erase extra sketch lines. Darken the final lines. Add color. Put a bit of green under his feet for grass.

He's really strutting his stuff!

Trash can

We need a place to put our trash. Let's draw a trash can!

1 Sketch an oval for the lid. Draw two curved lines under it to begin the can.

2 Draw four short, straight lines on top of the lid, to begin the handle. Draw a long curved line inside the lid oval. Draw a curved line for the bottom of the trash can.

3 Draw two curved lines, connecting to the straight lines, to complete the handle. Sketch two large ovals for eyes. Draw another oval for the nose. Draw a curved line to begin the mouth.

4 Draw two curved lines inside his eyes to make him squint.

5 Draw curved dotted lines above the trash can. Draw little hearts for flies. Draw two curved lines to make a tongue.

6 LOOK at the final drawing! Erase extra sketch lines. Darken the final lines. Add color.

Whew! She doesn't look happy smelling trash all day!

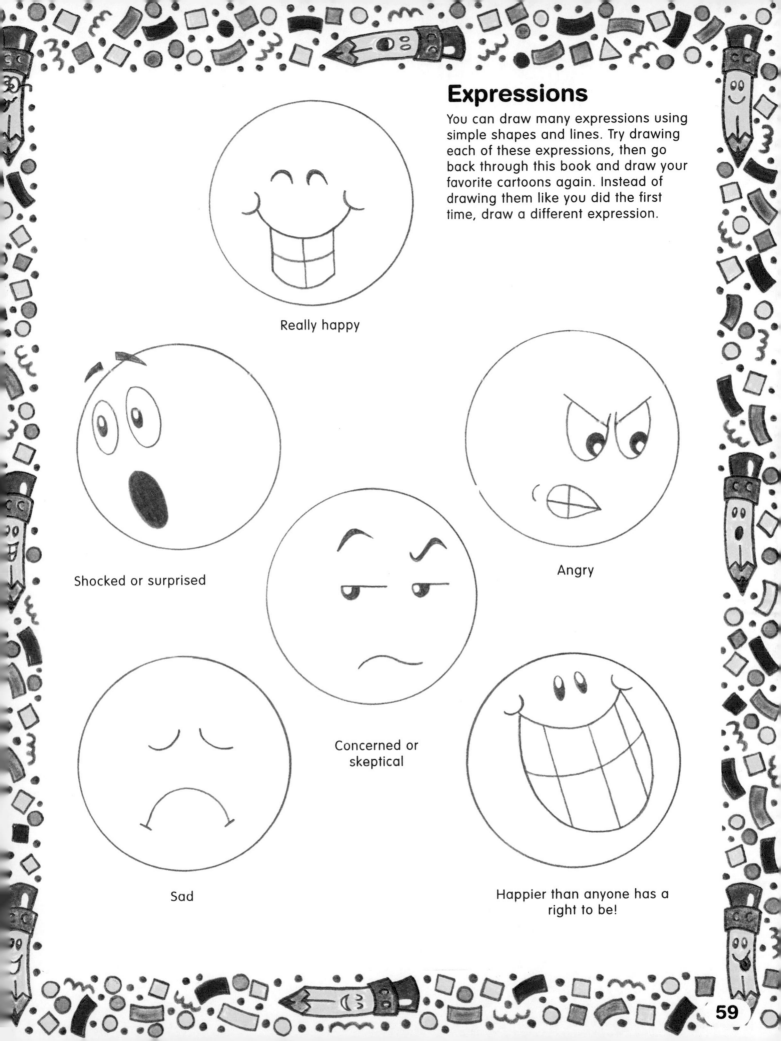

Expressions

You can draw many expressions using simple shapes and lines. Try drawing each of these expressions, then go back through this book and draw your favorite cartoons again. Instead of drawing them like you did the first time, draw a different expression.

Really happy

Shocked or surprised

Angry

Concerned or skeptical

Sad

Happier than anyone has a right to be!

More expressions

Look in a mirror. Think of an emotion. Make a face to match the emotion. LOOK closely at the shapes and lines on your face. Sketch the details you see.

Or, have a friend sit across the table from you. Make funny faces at each other and try to sketch the shapes and lines you see. It's fun and it will help you improve your drawing skills.

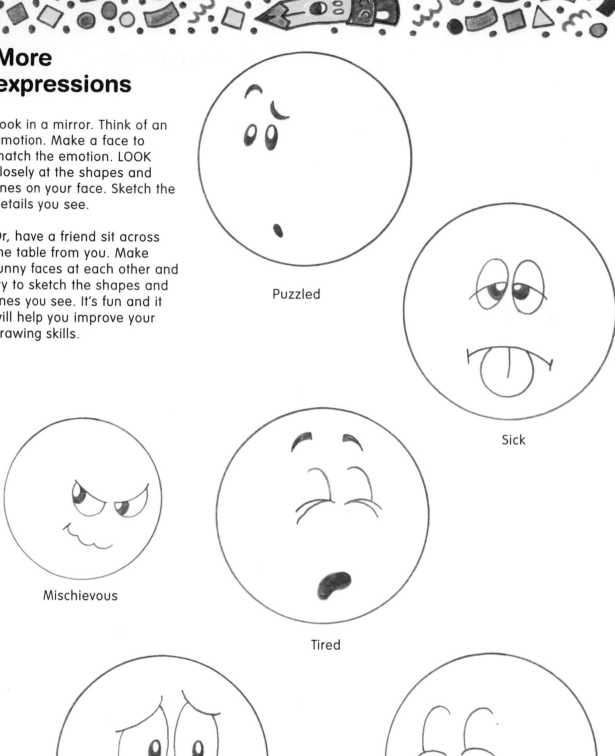

Puzzled

Sick

Mischievous

Tired

Worried

Content

Here are a couple more
examples of sketches and
finished drawings. Try them!

Remember, practice, practice, practice, and you will get better and better.

Look around you and find other things you can draw using simple lines and shapes.

62

Now you're ready to take off on your own! Use what you have learned in this book to turn any sort of object into a cartoon character. Draw two or three different characters and put them together in a scene. Which are happy? Which are sad, or angry, or confused? Can you turn them into a story?

Hmmm....

Award yourself! On the next page you'll find an award certificate you can photocopy to let the world know you're a **Cartoonist's Apprentice First Class!**

Have you enjoyed this book?

Find out about other books in this series and see sample pages online at

www.123draw.com

Cartoonist's Apprentice First Class

THIS IS TO CERTIFY THAT

HAS SUCCESSFULLY COMPLETED THE "1-2-3 DRAW COOL CARTOON STUFF" COURSE.

Steve Barr

INSTRUCTOR

DATE